Desert Safari

Enter the X·Zone!

Every **X·Zone** book is full of facts and amazing true stories that will take you around the world and back.

You'll find vivid photos and illustrations that will spark your imagination.

One thing to keep in mind: If you see a word in **bold**, look in the glossary for the meaning!

Ready for an adventure in reading? Then enter the **X·Zone!**

Contents

What is the largest desert in the world?
PAGE **2**

You wouldn't want to find this spider in your shoe!
PAGE **22**

What are the "ships of the desert"?
PAGE **22**

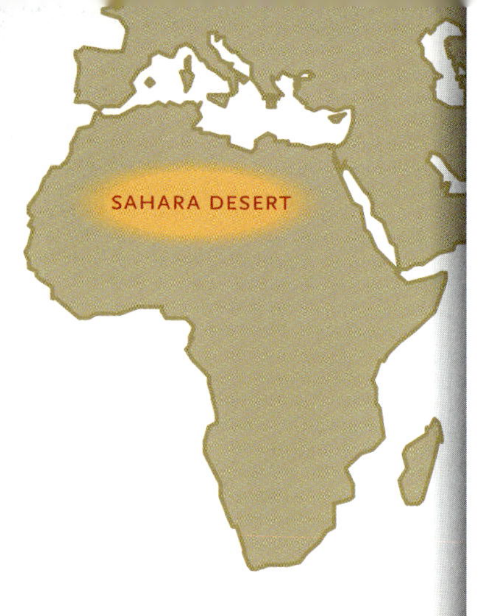

The Sahara only gets about 10 inches (254 millimeters) of rain a year. Some years it doesn't rain at all!

Close your eyes and imagine you are in the desert. What do you see? Camels, a prickly cactus, whitened animal bones? Or maybe a person lost and dying from thirst!

Well, my desert pal, Zack, and I are going to take you on a sandy adventure to the largest desert in the world: the Sahara in Africa.

I am going to share my safari travel journal with you. You will read about how a massive desert spider ended up in my shoe. And how we almost met up with a dust devil.

So, bring along your goggles and your imagination, and join me on a desert safari. Oh, and don't forget your hat—most days are over 122°F (50°C)! This is sure to be an adventure you will never forget.

A *Sea* of *Sand*

The desert can be a dangerous place, so it's good to know some facts before we set off. Some people go and never return!

Nestled in northern Africa, the Sahara is the largest desert in the world. It's been there a very long time—2.5 million years in fact. The word Sahara comes from the Arabic language and means desert. It takes up a mighty big space. Check out the map!

You'd wonder why anyone would want to live in a desert because it's such a hot, dry place. Well, plenty of people do. Around two million people call the Sahara home. Most people live near an **oasis** where there is water, so they can herd animals and farm. Others roam the desert, moving from place to place. They are known as **nomadic** people.

Zack is revving the engine. Get ready. We are off to Niger, the heart of the Sahara … oh, and just to warn you—watch out for the camel slobber!

Dear Diary,

This morning we left Niamey, the capital of Niger. We stocked up on canned food (lots of baked beans) and the most important items of all: **jerry cans** of water and fuel. We have a lot of them. Zack says it's better to be safe than sorry.

He says freak storms, snakebites, sunstroke, and even icy weather can all happen out here. So, we need to be prepared. In our survival kit we have some really cool stuff.

- Sand ladders are really important. We use them to put under the tires of the car to cross areas of very soft sand.

- Duct tape to fix any type of hole.

- Rope, in case we need to be towed.

- We also have this special type of glue to take out cactus thorns.

- The weirdest items are large plastic bags. They can be used to keep you dry in a sudden rainstorm, or to collect water. They can even be stuffed with leaves or cow dung to make nice warm blankets! Dried cow dung is available in the markets; it's cheap and has no odor.

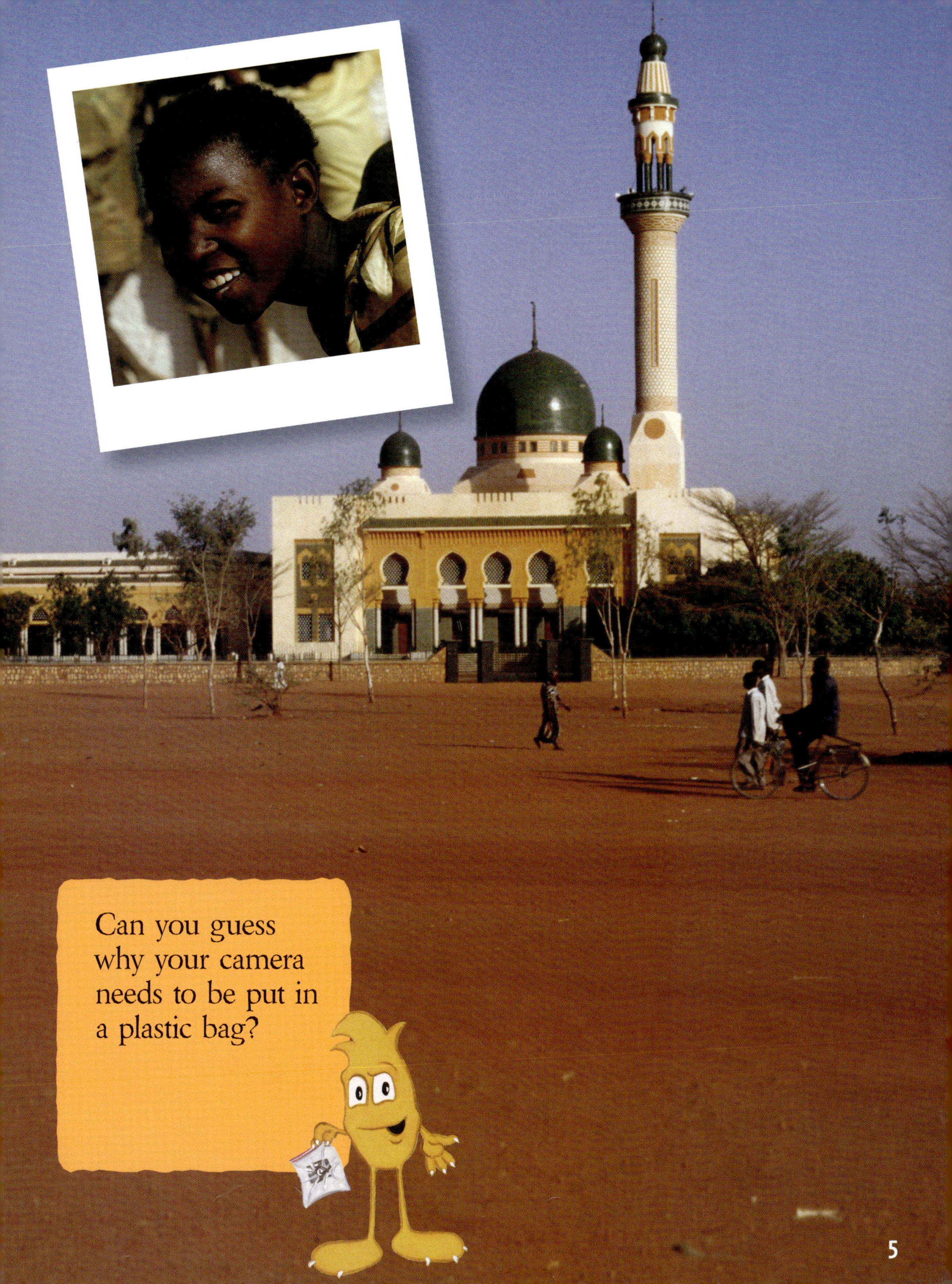

Can you guess
why your camera
needs to be put in
a plastic bag?

- Zack says everyone in the desert should carry a Swiss army knife.

- Zack packed some large mirrors. I asked him if he was planning on looking at himself a lot. But he explained they are used to flash rescuers if they are looking for us. And I mustn't forget my camera!

A Mouthful of Sand

Bumping along in the four wheel drive vehicle today, I must have swallowed half a bucket of sand at least! Not to mention that I could build a sandcastle with the sand inside my shoes. We spent most of the day surrounded by miles and miles of sand without another living thing in sight. It was weird, feeling so alone.

Later: We've just set up camp and it's time for a nap. Zack and I intend to stay up most of the night. We're going to check out some desert animals while they're out and about hunting for food. Most of them are **nocturnal**, so they come out of their underground burrows and tunnels at night when it's cool.

Dried cow dung

Zack was telling me about an amazing little tunnel-digger called a fennec fox. To escape the heat of the day, these critters burrow underground and then line their tunnels with grass. The tunnel can be around 3 feet (1 meter) deep, and 30 feet (9 meters) long. Wow! That's a lot of digging for a little fox! Zack showed me a photo. He said they have enormous ears that help them lose excess heat.

Later: Night is falling now, and after a scorching hot day of 113°F (45°C), it is starting to get very cold. Zack says it gets so cold in the desert at night because there's no moisture in the air, or plants and trees to trap and hold heat through the night. So, I've bundled up with a sweater and thick socks. The sun is setting and the sand is glowing a hot red color, like burning coals from a fire. It's beautiful. The eeriest thing is the silence. No wind, no cars, no people, and no sounds. I think I can hear my own heartbeat.

Zack and I are about to head out with our cameras on our animal search. Wish us luck. I'll write again in the morning.

Dear Diary,

Last night the desert seemed to come alive in front of our eyes. It was amazing. The desert animals that burrow underground in the daytime to keep cool appeared as if from nowhere. The desert sure is a different place at night.

The first animal to appear was a cute and spiky little critter called a desert hedgehog. It scurried around searching for insects until it spotted us and then curled up in a spiky ball—hoping to go unnoticed, I guess.

Farther ahead we saw a striped, sandy-colored animal **stalking** a small lizard. Zack whispered that it was a striped hyena and that there were lots of them around here.

In the distance I saw a large animal with huge horns. I tried to get a closer look, but it spotted me and took off. Zack said it was an antelope called an addax. It's one of the largest desert animals.

As we headed back to camp, Zack told me that most desert animals do not have to drink at all. They get all the water they need from food. Imagine that!

Morning:

I stepped out of my tent this morning and there on the sand were these weird swishy marks. I totally freaked out when Zack said they were the marks left by a desert snake.

While we ate our breakfast, Zack showed me his book about desert animals. He showed me a photo of a horned viper. I sure hope that wasn't the snake that swished by my tent last night. It's one of the most dangerous snakes in the world, and one drop of its **venom** can kill 200,000 mice! Yikes!

I'm sleeping with my flashlight on tonight to try and stop the animals and insects from coming close to me while I sleep.

13

DAY 2: NIGHT CRITTERS

After my heartbeat went back to normal, we headed off for our day's adventure. It was slow driving today; the sand was very soft. We let down the tire pressure instead of using the sand ladders. This gave us more grip on the sand.

Later in the afternoon we noticed lots of birds in the distance, circling around in the air. We drove closer and came across a massive dead lizard. The circling birds turned out to be some rather large and hungry-looking vultures. Zack told me the lizard was a desert monitor. His book says they have been on our planet for 130 million years and grow up to 5 feet (152 centimeters) long. That's nearly as tall as me! Apparently these critters can put up with very hot temperatures better than any other desert animal. Hmm, I wonder what this one died from. Just as we were leaving, we noticed a mean-looking jackal heading toward its lizard dinner!

Dear Diary,

We headed off at dawn today, before the heat set in. I decided to stop complaining about the heat after Zack showed me a photo of the desert marathon! Apparently every year around 700 people run a 140 mile (220 kilometer) marathon in the Sahara called the Marathon of the Sands. It can take up to a week—how crazy is that?

After a few short hours we rolled into an unusual mud-brick town called Agadez. All the houses were made of mud.

I felt excited because this is the meeting place for the Tuaregs, the people who live in this part of the desert. My first chance to meet some desert people—cool! They are also called the "blue men," as they wear blue clothes over their faces to protect them from evil spirits entering their mouths.

Zack said he had a surprise waiting for me at the Grand Marche. Hmmm …

The Grand Marche turned out to be the market place in town. It was so interesting. There were people selling silver, camel-hair blankets, leather bags, and even blocks of salt.

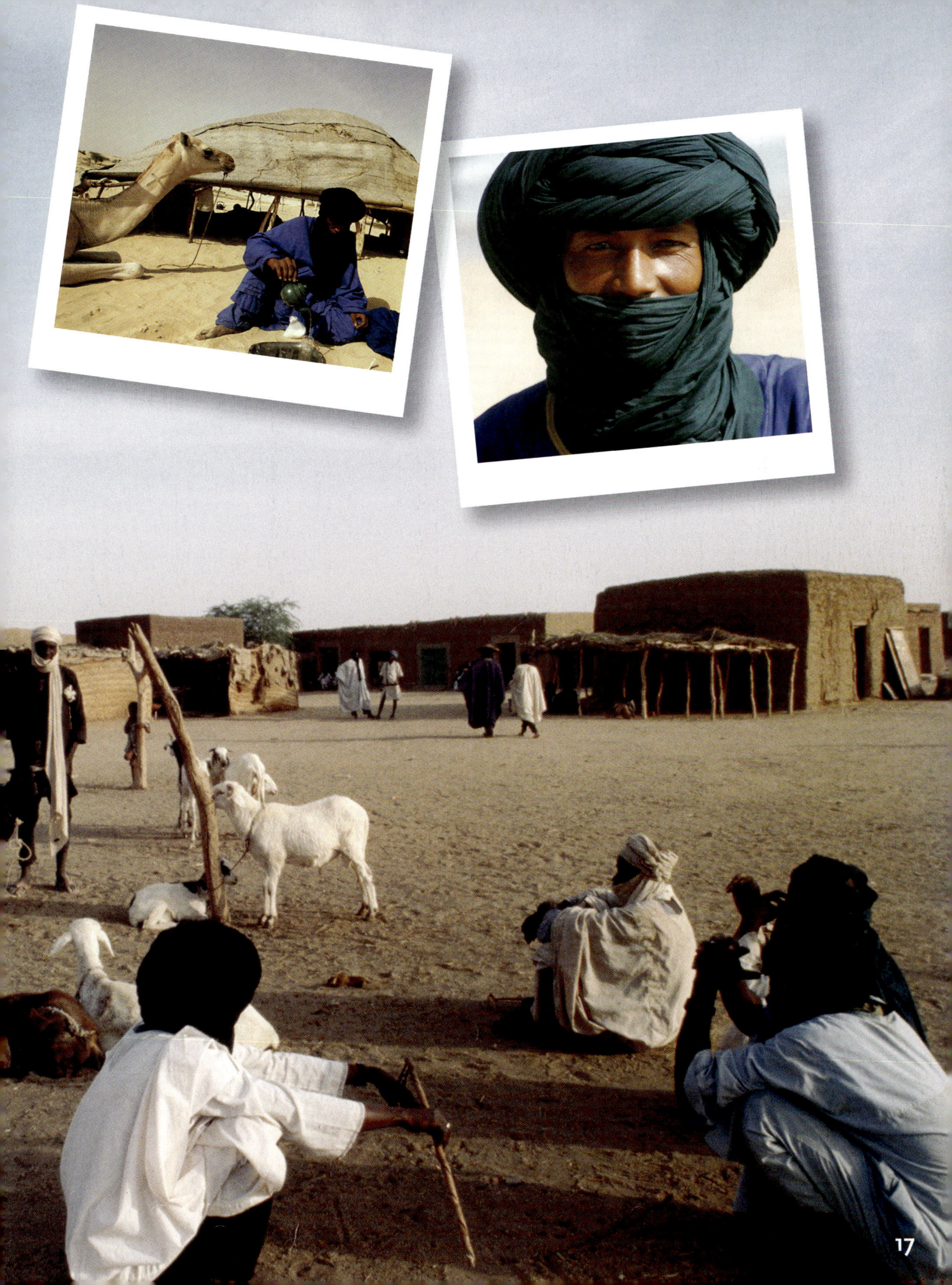

Then we came across my surprise. Can you believe it? … two camel drivers with their camels to take us on the rest of our safari. The camels were awesome. Their eyelashes were so long, you could hang your washing from them! I read up about them over lunch. These guys are amazing!

Here's what I found out.

In addition to their curly eyelashes, camels also have a third eyelid that acts like a windshield wiper and moves from side to side to wipe the sand away. Cool!

Camels can drink up to 25 percent of their body weight in a short time and store a large amount of water in their stomachs. They can go without water for 5–7 days.

Camels store fat in their humps, and they use it when food is scarce.

The hump flops to one side when a camel needs food; the hump will stand up again when the camel has eaten a good meal.

A baby camel is born without a hump. It has to start eating solid food before it can start developing one.

You might hug a friend to keep warm, but camels huddle together to keep cool. Their group body temperature is cooler than the air around them.

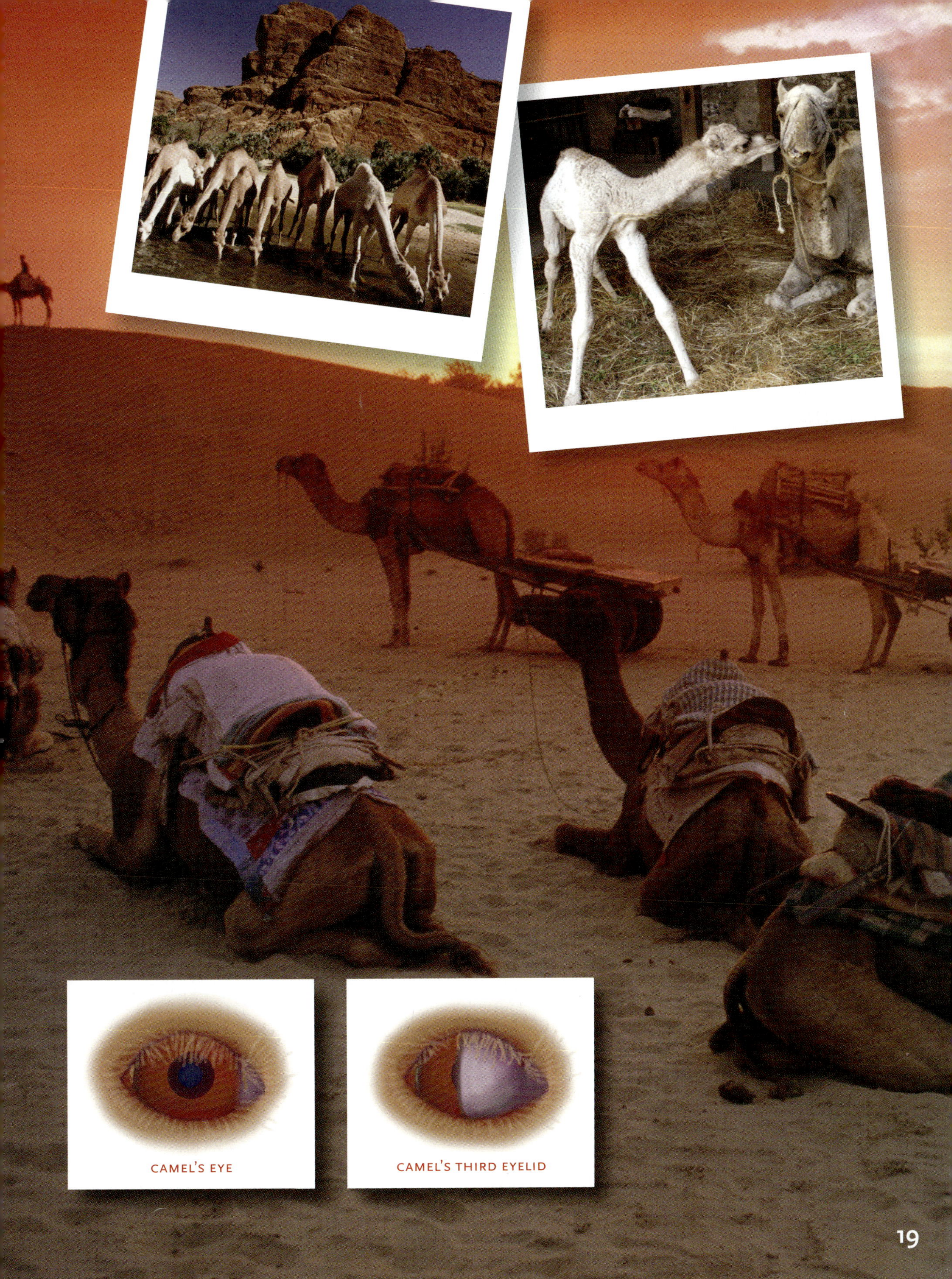
CAMEL'S EYE
CAMEL'S THIRD EYELID

The people of the Sahara use the camel not only for transportation, but also for milk, meat, wool, and shade. No wonder camels are so special to the desert people.

The afternoon was spent making our way on our camels up into the Air Mountains. The camel drivers sang as we went along. I wondered if there was anything called "camel sickness," I sure felt a bit queasy.

When we arrived we made camp under a starlit sky with a Tuareg tribe. They told us that the winds—*haboob* in Arabic—were coming, and the air would be filled with a choking dust. It sounded scary, but Zack did not seem too worried. Off to Timia tomorrow and . . . fresh water!

Dear Diary,

After a few hours traveling over rocky ground, I decided that camels are not the most comfortable form of transport. And they sure do slobber. But then at last, there it was! A green garden in the middle of the desert. At first I thought it was a **mirage**. It was full of palm trees, orange trees, and … a waterfall. An oasis! I could not wait to take off my shoes and leap under the waterfall. Taking a shower has never felt so good!

As I was putting on my shoes, ready to head off again, I felt a furry tickle from inside my shoe. Yikes! I threw the shoe off and there, crawling out of it, was the largest spider I have ever seen! Its body was about the size of a human hand. It must have been hiding there to escape the heat. Zack said it was a camel spider. They eat scorpions, lizards, other spiders, and birds. Gulp!

We climbed aboard our camels, "the ships of the desert," and sadly left our oasis. Our mission was to reach the Tenere, the most beautiful part of the whole Sahara. The Tenere is about the size of Switzerland. All around us were sparkling white sand dunes built by the wind. They change shape all the time and travel across the desert as they are blown by the wind. They can move up to 66 feet (20 meters) a year.

Speaking of wind, it sure is getting windy. The sand keeps getting in my eyes. It's time to set up camp for the night. We're going to need shelter!

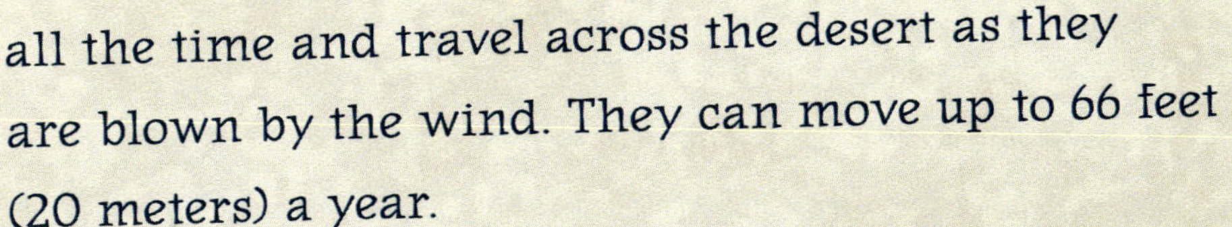

The water for an oasis comes up from an underground river.

Dear Diary,

We camped at the base of a sand dune last night. It was huge, and its shadow protected us from the morning sun. The wind blew and the sand hummed around us. It seemed like the sand was making music. I wrapped my head in a scarf, leaving only a small slit for my eyes to see through. The wind was becoming stronger and the sand felt like it was cutting my skin. Zack looked worried, which made me nervous too. He grabbed the binoculars, looked toward the horizon, and let out a gasp. It was a dust devil and it was heading our way. I'd read about dust devils. The people of the desert fear them. The Tuareg tribe warned us that we might encounter something like this.

They are like fierce whirlwinds that can reach half a mile into the air. They toss sand, dust, and even small animals into the air.

It was time to head for the safety of Agadez and, sadly, the end of our desert safari. As we turned the camels around, I took my last photos of the sand swirling on top of the sand dunes. It was a sight I will never forget.

Dust devils are also found on the planet Mars

Interview

Simon Wilkinson is a photographer who enjoys traveling the world visiting interesting places, especially deserts.

 **Which deserts in the world have you been to?**

I've been visiting Australia's deserts since 1981 when I was a student at Durham University in England. I joined an expedition to the Great Sandy Desert in Western Australia. Other deserts I've spent time in are the Turkana (Northern Frontier District) of Kenya, and some of the **arid** parts of the southwestern United States, such as Arizona and Death Valley in California.

 **Are they all different?**

Deserts are much more varied than most people imagine. The most widely accepted definition of a desert is anywhere that the average annual rainfall is less than 10 inches (250 mm). Apart from obvious places like the Sahara in Africa, you might be surprised to learn that this definition also includes most of Antarctica! Some deserts have a very rocky terrain. In fact, deserts with huge sand dunes are much less common than is generally thought.

What was your most worrying thought going to a desert?

In Australian deserts—snakes! Coming from England where we only have one mildly venomous snake (the adder), I imagined that we'd be tripping over some of the most venomous land snakes in the world every day. Actually it is quite rare to see snakes by accident— you usually have to go looking for them with someone who knows about their **habitats**. Having said that, Sue, a friend of mine who is really scared of snakes, had a very unnerving experience. She had a death adder slither under her camp chair while we were in the Great Victoria Desert in Australia.

Q **Do you have any good tips for people visiting a desert?**

A It depends on the location of the desert, but generally speaking:

- Protect yourself from the sun. The thinning of the **ozone layer** means the sun is more damaging that it was even 20 years ago.
- Wear good-quality walking boots.
- Take a good-quality sleeping bag—desert nights can get very cold.
- Drink lots of water, especially in the early part of your desert trip when your body hasn't adapted to the new conditions. If you're in a **remote** place make sure you take enough food, water, and fuel to last the distance. Water is especially important. You can survive a long time without food, but as little as 2 days without water in high temperatures.

Q **Have you ever come across anything dangerous in the desert?**

A I was unlucky enough to have been stung by a scorpion while in Kenya, Africa. It was definitely the most painful thing I've ever experienced. It's the only time I can remember literally screaming from pain. It happened while I was asleep. The scorpion somehow got through my mosquito net and stung me on the back of my knee. It was 3 days before the pain had subsided enough for me to be able to do anything.

Quiz

1. How old is the Sahara?
   a) 100 years old
   b) 300 years old
   c) 2.5 million years old
   d) 5 million years old

2. The word *Sahara* comes from Arabic and means *desert*.
   True/False

3. How many people live in the Sahara?
   a) around 2 million
   b) around 5 million
   c) around 300
   d) around 2,000

4. How many inches of rain does the Sahara get per year?
   a) around 5 inches
   b) around 50 inches
   c) around 20 inches
   d) around 10 inches

5. What are mirrors in a survival kit used for?
   a) signaling rescuers
   b) attracting animals
   c) burning insects for food
   d) checking yourself for sunburn

6. A desert monitor is
   a) a person who spends his time studying the desert
   b) part of a computer system that tracks desert weather patterns
   c) a tough, heat-resistant, and ancient type of lizard
   d) a river that runs underneath the desert

7. What is the name of the mud city in the Sahara?
   a) Niger
   b) Morocco
   c) Agadez
   d) Niamey

8. Camels store food in their
   a) long legs
   b) necks
   c) humps
   d) mouths

9. How does a sand dune travel across the desert?
   a) rain washes it away
   b) the wind blows the sand
   c) they don't move at all
   d) the sun melts the sand

10. What is a dust devil?
    a) a type of animal
    b) a hole in the ground filled with dust
    c) a type of cloud in the desert
    d) a whirlwind that occurs in the desert

Answers

1 True
2 c)
3 a)
4 d)
5 a)
6 c)
7 c)
8 c)
9 b)
10 d)

Glossary

arid Very dry region and without enough rain for plants to grow.

habitats Natural surroundings where a particular type of animal or plant lives or grows.

jerry cans Flat-sided cans for storing or transporting liquids, especially gasoline or water.

mirage An optical illusion (false impression) of a sheet of water appearing in the desert or on a hot road.

nocturnal Active at night.

nomadic Groups of people who move from one place to another rather than living in one place all of the time.

oasis A place in a desert where there is water and therefore plants and trees and sometimes a village or town.

ozone layer Is that part of the Earth's stratosphere containing a high concentration of ozone.

remote Far away from civilization or any other populated area.

stalking Following an animal as closely as possible without being seen or heard.

venom Poisonous liquid which some animals produce usually by biting or stinging.

Index